Usborne
Travel
Games Pad

Written by Simon Tudhope and Sam Smith

Designed by Marc Maynard and Karen Tomlins

Edited by Sam Taplin

Airshow acrobatics

1

Which smoke plume must the jet's pilot follow to perform the same stunts as the first plane and then land behind it?

FINISH

Travel bingo

How quickly can you spot all the things shown below? Cross each one off once you've seen it. To play with a friend, give them the travel bingo from page 22, and race to see who completes their list first.

Red car

SUPERSAVE

Supermarket

Bird

Road repairs

Satellite dish

Statue

Tractor

Bicycle

Service station

Pair them up

Turn to page 184 for instructions on how to play this game.

3

Circles and squares

Write all the numbers 1 to 9 in the grid, so the four squares around each circle add up to that circle's total, and the red, green and blue squares add up to the totals at the bottom. One number has been filled in for you.

Scavenger hunt

Try to spot all these things on your journey and mark them off as you go.

○ House

○ Motorcycle

○ Crane

○ Green car

○ Plane

○ Gate

○ Dog

○ Police car

○ Traffic cone

○ Service station

○ Bench

○ Horse

○ Puddle

○ Tree

○ Ambulance

○ Store

○ Silver car

○ Concrete mixer

○ Statue

○ Road sign

Taxi dash

Draw a line from the taxi to the airport as fast as you can without driving off the road.

Boxes

7

Turn to page 179 for instructions on how to play this game.

Memory squares

Study this page for one minute, trying to remember which pictures are in which squares. Then turn the page and see if you can fill in the blanks correctly.

Memory squares

Look at the previous page to find out how to play this game.

Regions

Turn to page 181 for instructions on how to play this game.

Explorers quiz

Q1. Whose expedition was the first to reach the South Pole?
a) Robert Scott   b) Roald Amundsen   c) Edmund Hillary

Q2. In a book by C.S. Lewis, where did four children find an entrance to Narnia: down a rabbit hole **or** at the back of a wardrobe?

Q3. What name was given to the place where Captain James Cook first landed in Australia?
a) Botany Bay   b) Bondi Beach   c) Cook Cove

Q4. Who led the first expedition to sail around the world but died along the way:
Christopher Columbus **or**
Ferdinand Magellan?

Q5. Which European explorer ended up serving in the court of Kublai Khan in China?
a) Hernán Cortés   b) Walter Raleigh   c) Marco Polo

Q6. Who first discovered North America?
a) the Portuguese   b) the Chinese   c) the Vikings

Q7. In which ship did Sir Francis Drake sail around the world?
a) *Golden Fleece*   b) *Golden Hind*   c) *Golden Horn*

Strike out

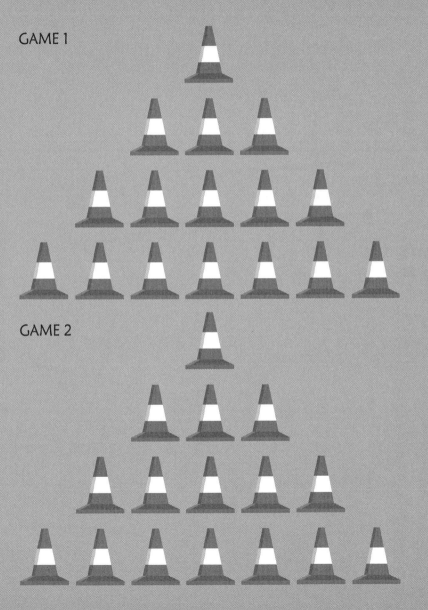

Turn to page 182 for instructions on how to play this game.

GAME 1

GAME 2

Os and Xs

This is a game for two players, played on a 3x3 grid. Player 1 uses Os and Player 2 uses Xs. Take turns drawing your symbol in an empty square. The winner is the player who draws three of their symbols in a straight line. If neither player gets three in a row, the game is a draw.

Fortune teller

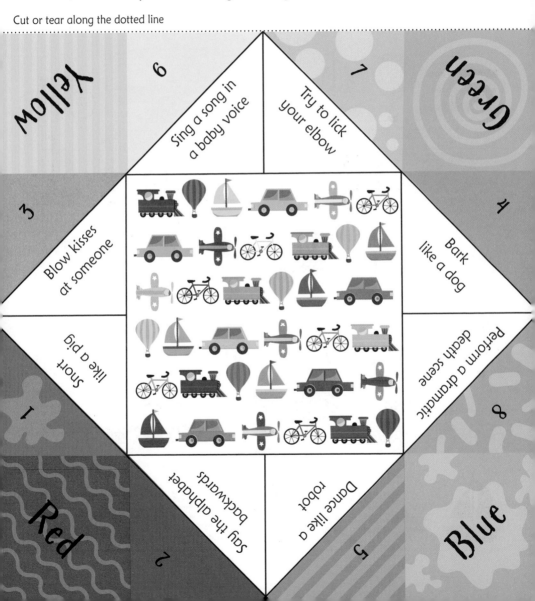

13

Turn to page 191 for instructions on how to fold this page into a fortune teller, then let it pick dares for you and your friends.

Cut or tear along the dotted line

Yellow

6

Sing a song in a baby voice

Try to lick your elbow

7

Green

3

Blow kisses at someone

Bark like a dog

4

Snort like a pig

Perform a dramatic death scene

1

8

Say the alphabet backwards

Dance like a robot

Red

2

5

Blue

Fortune teller

Spot the difference

Can you find and circle **six** differences between the two sailing scenes below?

The road

Turn to page 180 for instructions on how to play this game.

Cycle climb

Guide the cyclist along a clear path up
the mountain roads to the race's finish.

FINISH

START

Stepping stones

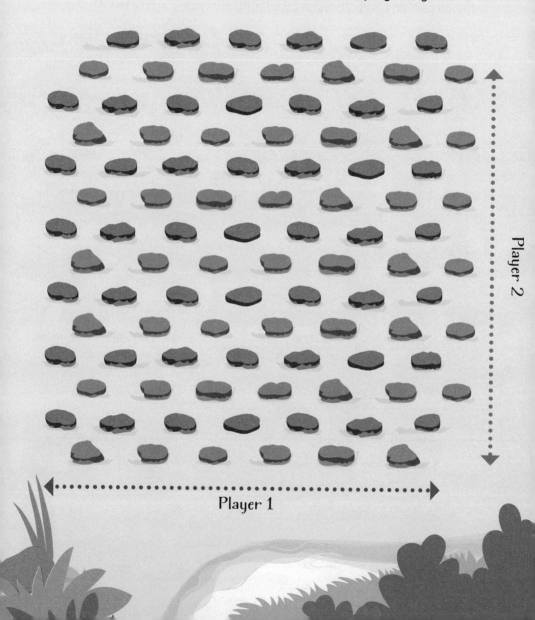

Turn to page 178 for instructions on how to play this game.

Player 2

Player 1

Seaside squiggles

18

Can you turn these squiggles into things you might see at the beach?

Outside the window

1. Plate messages

Use the letters in a vehicle's plate to make up
the silliest phrase you can. For example, WMGC
could stand for "Woman Marries Giant Cornflake."

WMGC

H4-CM

2. Sign rhymes

Look out for a place name sign, then think of a rhyming phrase
to go with it. For example, with Queen's Square you could say:
"For Queen's Square, follow the bear". See who can come up
with the funniest rhyme.

3. What's your car?

Pick a number between 10 and 20, then
count all the cars that pass your window
until you reach your number. That's the
car you'll have when you're older!

16

4. Who lives there?

In this game, one person looks for an interesting house. When they see
one, they ask "Who lives there?" Everyone takes turns describing who
the owners might be. For example, are the owners old? Do they have
any pets? What are their hobbies?

Car parts

Circle the group of parts that can be put together to make the car shown on the right.

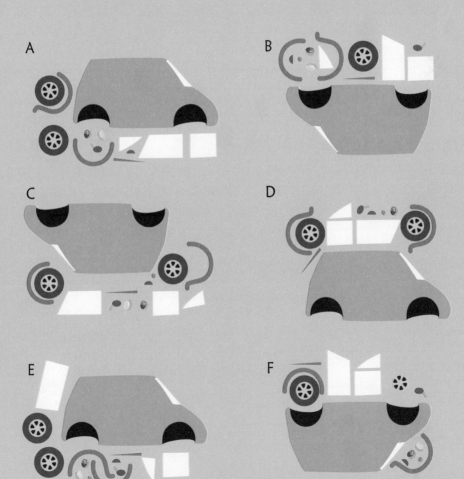

A

B

C

D

E

F

Word maker

How many new words can you make in two minutes, using the nine letters of the word below? Once the time is up, add up the total score of all your words – a two letter word scores two points, a three letter word scores three points, and so on.

m o u n t a i n s

Words	Points	Words	Points
....	......	....	......
....	......	....	......
....	......	....	......
....	......	....	......
....	......	....	......
		....	......
		....	......

TOTAL = ...

Travel bingo

How quickly can you spot all the things shown below? Cross each one off once you've seen it. To play with a friend, give them the travel bingo from page 2, and race to see who completes their list first.

Concrete mixer

Blue car

Traffic cone

Bridge

Stop sign

Cow

Motorcycle

Forest

River

Safari search

Find the names of all the animals at the bottom in the grid below.

```
S T G M F Y E K N O M
N O P E R U T L U V T
A S R L H C I E R E N
K T H E I O G F E L A
L R D P C N L F K I H
E I R H I O I A A D P
K C A A V P N R N O E
A H P N R N E I Z C Z
N R O T O B O G H O A
S Z E I R A E C I R L
T G L N I O L Z H C G
```

ZEBRA LEOPARD LION CROCODILE SNAKE VULTURE
MONKEY RHINOCEROS OSTRICH ELEPHANT GIRAFFE

Hexagon

Turn to page 187 for instructions on how to play this game.

Statue maker

To make a statue with a friend, tear out this page and fold along the dotted lines. Hiding it from your friend, draw the bottom part on the plinth, then fold it over for them to draw the top part. Unfold to see your statue!

City sudoku

This grid is made up of six blocks, each made up of six squares. Fill in the blank squares so that every row, column and block contains all six of the symbols shown below.

Treasure hunter

Turn to page 189 for instructions on how to play this game.

Cut or tear along the dotted line.

Quick-fire ten

This is a game for two or more people.

1. One person thinks of a category of things, such as countries, famous people, vehicles, animals or kinds of food.

2. The other person has to think of ten things in that category in one minute. If they succeed, they get one point.

3. Take turns being the one who thinks of the category. The first person to five points is the winner.

Animals!

TIP: Some categories are easier than others – for example, "food" is easy because there are lots of kinds of food. If you want to make a game harder, choose a category with fewer things in it, such as "water sports" or "vegetables that aren't green".

Tongue twisters

Who can say these tongue twisters the fastest?

1. Any noisy noise annoys an Ulster oyster on the coast,
   But an annoying noisy noise annoys any oyster most.

2. She sells seashells on the seashore.
   The shells she sells are seashells, I'm sure.
   For if she sells seashells on the seashore,
   the shells she sells are surely seashore shells.

3. Many an anemone meets an enemy anemone.

4. Selfish shellfish... Selfish shellfish... Selfish shellfish...

5. How many clams can a clan of clams cram
   in a clam clan's clean cream can?

6. Sam swan swam over the sea – Swim, Sam swan, swim!
   Sam swan swam back again. Well swum, Sam swan!

Turn to page 180 for instructions on how to play this game.

Parking puzzle

In the parked cars below, draw squares around the two sets of nine cars that match the sets on the right.

1

2

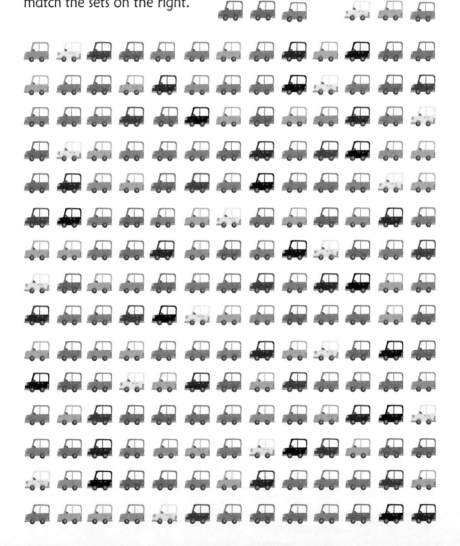

Travel bingo

How quickly can you spot all the things shown below? Cross each one off once you've seen it. To play with a friend, give them the travel bingo from page 48, and race to see who completes their list first.

Boat

Roof rack

Flower

Parking area

Fire truck

Picnic table

Campsite

Traffic cone

Golf course

Paper golf

Turn to page 186 for instructions on how to play this game.

Tee

Vehicle snap

This is a game for two or more people.

The object of this game is to spot pairs of vehicles at the same time, or within a short time of each other.

• For an easy game, look for, say, two blue cars, or two silver cars.

• For a harder game, try to spot two vehicles that are also the same type, such as two red sports cars, two blue trucks and so on, within five minutes of each other.

• For an even harder game, try to spot two vehicles that are exactly the same model, too, in a five-minute window.

Whoever manages to spot the most pairs of vehicles on your journey is the winner.

Maze master

Turn to page 190 for instructions on how to play this game.

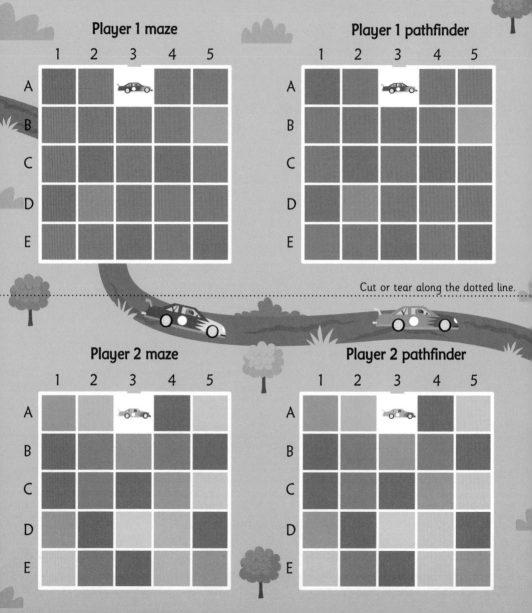

Player 1 maze

	1	2	3	4	5
A					
B					
C					
D					
E					

Player 1 pathfinder

	1	2	3	4	5
A					
B					
C					
D					
E					

Cut or tear along the dotted line.

Player 2 maze

	1	2	3	4	5
A					
B					
C					
D					
E					

Player 2 pathfinder

	1	2	3	4	5
A					
B					
C					
D					
E					

Target

Turn to page 183 for instructions on how to play this game.

Carousel cases

Direct the bags along the correct path on the carousel to reach the people waiting for them at the bottom.

20 questions

This is a game for two or more people.

1. One person thinks of something for everyone else to try to identify.

2. The other players take turns to ask a question about it – but no more than 20 questions can be asked in total. The questions can only be answered with "Yes" or "No" so they need to be things like "Has it got wings?" or "Does it live in the rainforest?"

3. If someone thinks they know what the thing is, they can guess at any time, but the guess counts as one of the 20 questions. If they are right, they have won, but if not, they are out of the game.

4. If no one guesses what it is by the time 20 questions have been asked, the person who thought of it has won.

Is it furry?

Does it swim?

Is it a snake?

No, no and yes!

Camping out

Campers often avoid pitching their tents too close together. In this game, two players take turns to mark a square for a tent. A tent cannot be drawn in any of the squares around another tent, including diagonals. The first player who can't go loses.

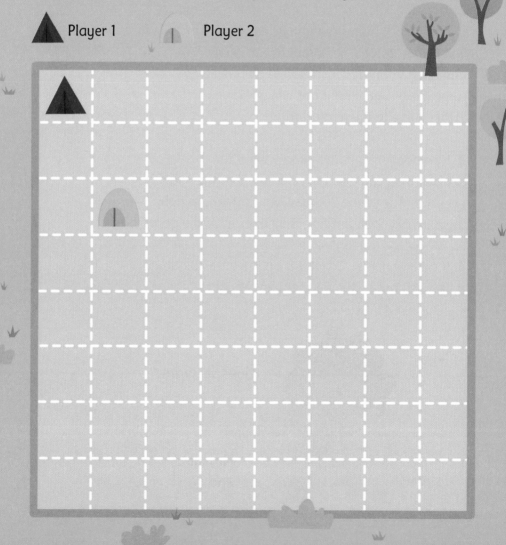

Player 1   Player 2

Spotting sounds

This is a game for two or more people.

1. Each person chooses something to spot and makes a silly noise to go with it. The noise shouldn't have anything to do with the thing that you've chosen, so don't choose anything as obvious as saying "woof" when you see a dog.

2. Each time someone spots their chosen thing, they make the noise that goes with it.

3. Everyone has to guess what each other is spotting, and the game ends when they have all been guessed.

TIP: If you're playing this in a car, don't make your noises too loud or sudden, in case you distract the driver. Try not to disturb other passengers on a train, ferry or plane either.

Four in a row

Turn to page 185 for instructions on how to play this game.

Geography quiz

Q1. Which is the only continent that doesn't have a desert?
a) Antarctica   b) Europe   c) North America

Q2. How are you most likely to be greeted in Montreal, Canada?
a) Hello   b) Bonjour   c) Hola

Q3. Put these countries in order from north to south.
a) Fiji   b) Norway   c) Mongolia

**Q4. Whose tomb was found
in the Valley of the Kings?**
a) Julius Caesar
b) Solomon
c) Tutankhamun

**Q5. If you stepped east across the International Date Line,
would you go back one day or forward one day?**

Q6. Which of these is NOT a real place?
a) Valhalla   b) Timbuktu   c) Zanzibar

**Q7. What are the summer storms that provide 80%
of India's yearly rainfall?**
a) monsoons   b) typhoons   c) cyclones

Circles and squares

43

Write all the numbers 1 to 9 in the grid, so the four squares around each circle add up to that circle's total, and the green, yellow and purple squares add up to the totals at the bottom. One number has been filled in for you.

Fizzbuzz

This is a game for two or more people.

1. Everyone takes turns to say numbers, counting up. So the first player starts by saying "one", the next player says "two", and so on.

2. If a number can be divided by **three**, say "**fizz**" instead of that number.

19

3. If a number can be divided by **five**, say "**buzz**" instead of that number.

buzz!

4. When a number can be divided by both **three and five**, say "**fizzbuzz**".

fizz!

5. If a player makes a mistake, they drop out of the game. The last person left counting is the winner.

Shoreline challenge

Can you guide the crab between the rocks to the refreshing pool below?

Stepping stones

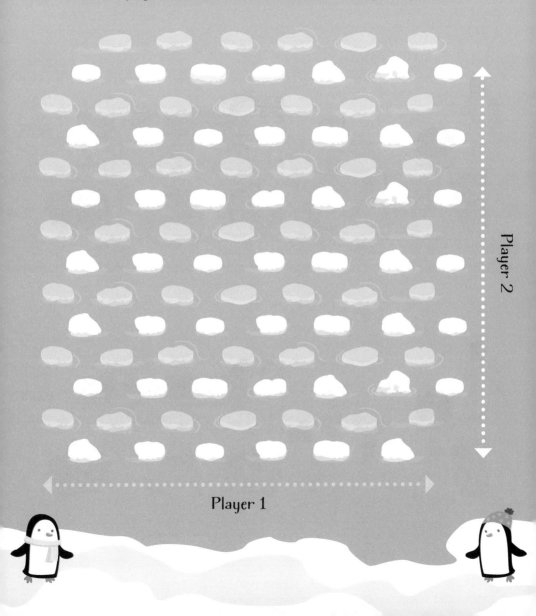

46

Turn to page 178 for instructions on how to play this game.

Player 2

Player 1

Spot the difference

47

Can you find and circle **six** differences between the two airport scenes below?

Travel bingo

How quickly can you spot all the things shown below? Cross each one off once you've seen it. To play with a friend, give them the travel bingo from page 32, and race to see who completes their list first.

Train crossing

Tow truck

Hills

Wooden fence

House

Concrete mixer

Clock

Bench

Clouds

Treasure hunter

Turn to page 189 for instructions on how to play this game.

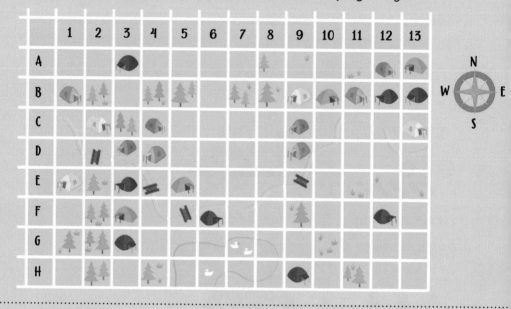

Cut or tear along the dotted line.

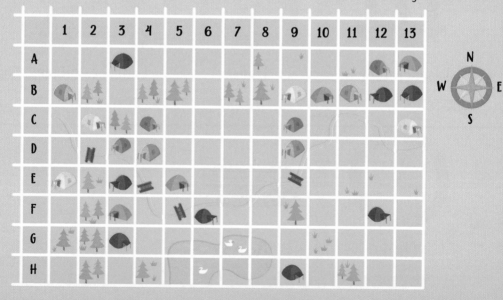

Vehicle sudoku

This grid is made up of six blocks, each made up of six squares. Fill in the blank squares so that every row, column and block contains all six of the vehicle symbols shown below.

Scavenger hunt

Try to spot all these things on your journey and mark them off as you go.

- ◯ Balloon
- ◯ Bicycle
- ◯ Crane
- ◯ Bridge
- ◯ Horse
- ◯ Green car
- ◯ Traffic signals
- ◯ Motorcycle
- ◯ Wind turbine
- ◯ Truck

- ◯ Service station
- ◯ Tractor
- ◯ Plane
- ◯ Tree
- ◯ Helicopter
- ◯ Bird
- ◯ Police car
- ◯ House
- ◯ Statue
- ◯ Red car

Packing list

Simon is packing to go on a trip. Memorize the items on his list for one minute, then turn the page to see the items he's going to put in his suitcase. What's missing? Check the list to see if your answer is correct.

1. Sunglasses
2. Map
3. T-shirt
4. Hat
5. Shoes
6. Rollerblades
7. Toothbrush
8. Sandals
9. Sunscreen
10. Shorts

Packing list

Turn the page over to find out how to do this puzzle.

Answers:

Obstruction

53

Turn to page 188 for instructions on how to play this game.

Quick draw

54

Draw a line as quickly as you can from the rocket to the red planet without straying from the planned flight path.

FINISH

Don't say "YES" or "NO"

This is a game for two or more people.

1. Everyone asks one player questions to which "yes" or "no" is the obvious answer. For example, they might ask "Are you 100 years old?"

2. The person being questioned must answer honestly, without saying "yes" or "no". In this example, they might say "Of course not!"

3. The game continues until the player being questioned makes a mistake and says "yes" or "no". Then it becomes their turn to question someone else.

Is your name Jenny?

Erm... it is.

TIP: Try asking a question that needs a long answer, followed by one where "yes" or "no" is the easiest answer. If you do this, you may find it easier to trick them.

Word maker

How many new words can you make in two minutes, using the ten letters of the word below? Once the time is up, add up the total score of all your words – a two letter word scores two points, a three letter word scores three points, and so on.

rainforest

Words	Points	Words	Points
....	......	....	......
....	......	....	......
....	......	....	......
....	......	....	......
....	......	....	......
		....	......
		....	......

TOTAL = ...

Sand search

57

Scan the grid for all the seaside words at the bottom.

```
G S P V S H A W E T L
U Y H D N O B F I S H
L A B E F C Y P A U K
L G N E L Q M N P E B
F T O W E L D V G I X
H S G A P C O C U S R
S O F E A Z N R L E B
C D I S E Y V A M V H
W O T E K C U B D A G
Y L P A F V E R T W S
E T A E L B B E P H T
```

CRAB SANDCASTLE PEBBLE BUCKET SHELL
SEAWEED FISH GULL WAVES TOWEL

Car silhouettes

Write each car's number beneath the silhouette that matches it.

1

2

3

4

5

6

7

8

9

10

11

12

A............

B............

C............

D............

E............

F............

G............

H............

I............

J............

K............

L............

Regions

Turn to page 181 for instructions on how to play this game.

Travel bingo

How quickly can you spot all the things shown below? Cross each one off once you've seen it. To play with a friend, give them the travel bingo from page 70, and race to see who completes their list first.

Bicycle

Forest

Bus

House

Concrete mixer

Clouds

Lake

Wooden fence

Boat

Four in a row

Turn to page 185 for instructions on how to play this game.

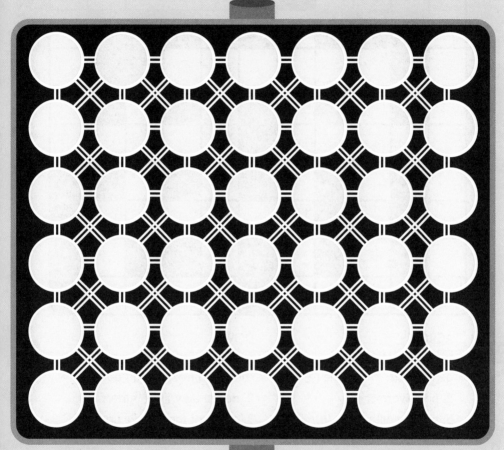

Skiing crossword

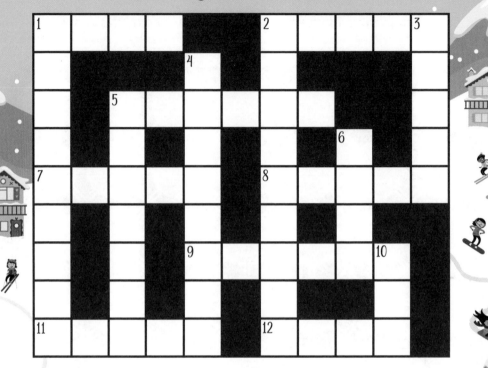

ACROSS

1. type of skiing with lots of aerial tricks: ____style (4)

2. neck-warmer (5)

5. ski race with gates (6)

7. another name for a piste or run: ski _____ (5)

8. footwear for the slopes: ski _____ (5)

9. skiers' holiday home (6)

11. Swiss Alpine mountain famed for its sheer north face (5)

12. Air resistance (4)

DOWN

1. serious medical condition caused by frozen body parts (9)

2. ridden by winter 'surfers' (9)

3. a pair of these make up the gates in a 5 across (5)

4. catch this to the top of a ski slope (5, 3)

5. sport of sliding across ice (7)

6. skiing stick (4)

10. unit measuring the warmth of winter clothing, and bedding (3)

Who am I?

This is a game for two or more people.

1. One player thinks of a person that everyone will know, for example, Robin Hood or Cinderella.

I'm Robin Hood.

2. They then give the others a clue, like this:

I rob the rich to feed the poor.

Each person has one guess. If someone gets it right, it's their turn to think of a person for the others to guess. If no one guesses correctly, the first person gives another clue:

I live in Sherwood Forest.

3. The game continues until someone guesses the mystery person, or until ten clues have been given. If no one gets it right, the first person tells everyone who it was, then thinks of someone else for them to guess.

Across the ice

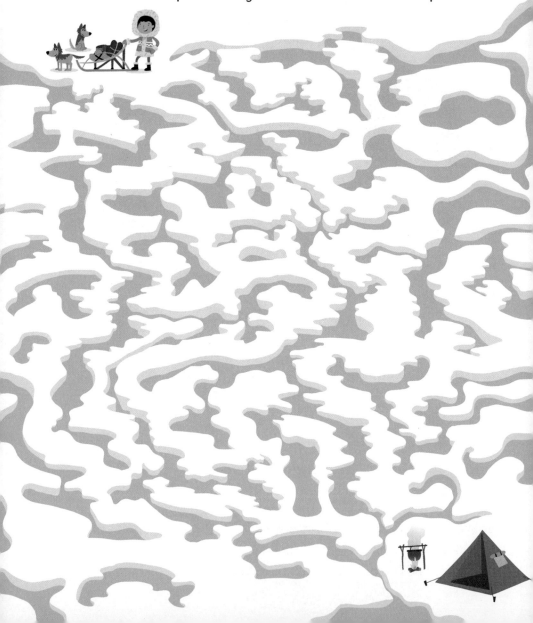

Guide the explorer safely back over the ice to his camp.

Hexagon

Turn to page 187 for instructions on how to play this game.

Four in a row

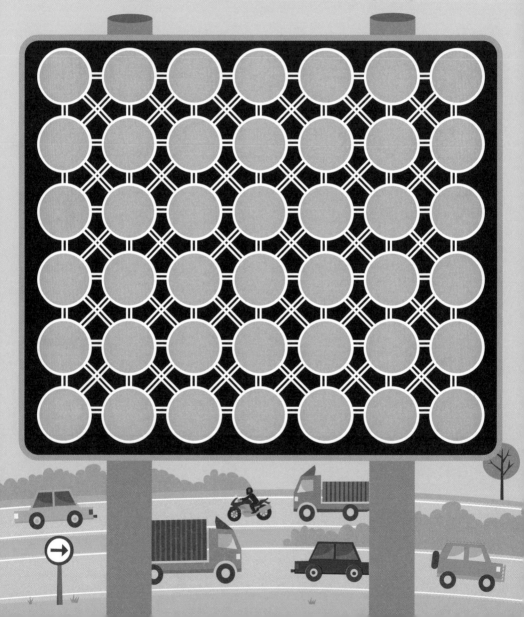

Turn to page 185 for instructions on how to play this game.

Pair them up

Turn to page 184 for instructions on how to play this game.

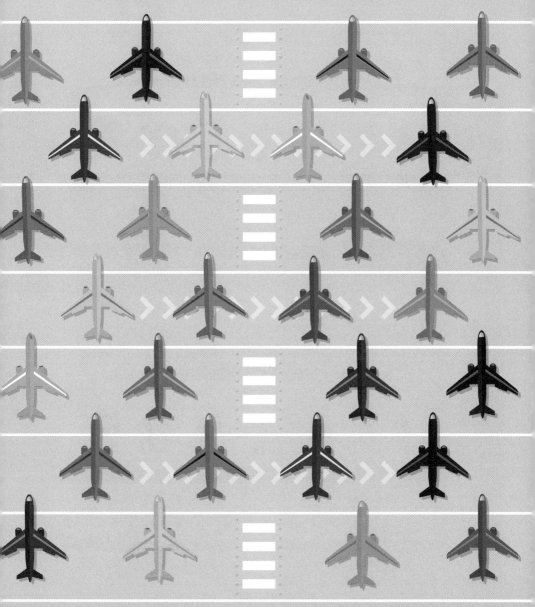

Spot the difference

Can you find and circle **six** differences between the two scenes below?

Train track

Guide the train along the right track to the station, picking up the people waiting at the platform on the way.

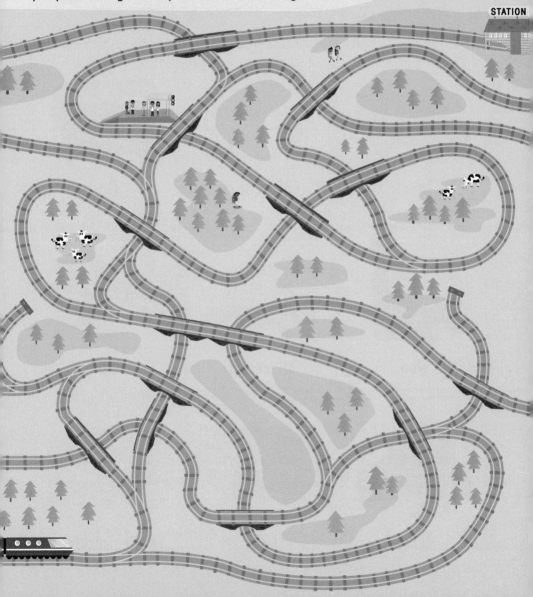

STATION

Travel bingo

How quickly can you spot all the things shown below? Cross each one off once you've seen it. To play with a friend, give them the travel bingo from page 60, and race to see who completes their list first.

Truck

Coffee shop

Bus

Dog

Silver car

Plane

Farm

Lake

Police station

Maze master

Turn to page 190 for instructions on how to play this game.

Player 1 maze

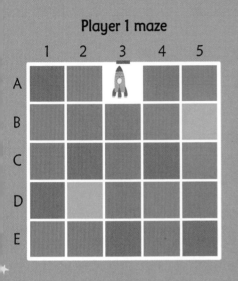

Player 1 pathfinder

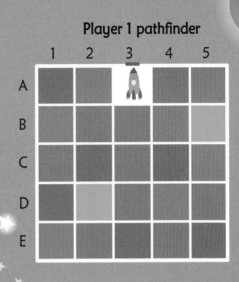

Cut or tear along the dotted line.

Player 2 maze

Player 2 pathfinder

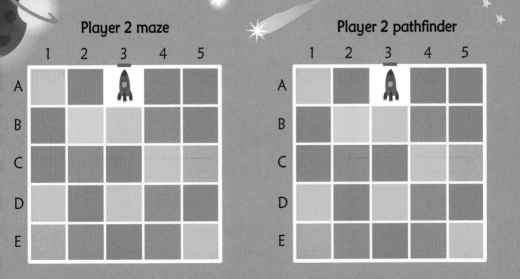

Treasure hunter

Turn to page 189 for instructions on how to play this game.

Cut or tear along the dotted line.

Memory story

This is a game for two or more people.

1. One person begins a story by making up a short sentence and saying it out loud.

One morning, Joe set out on a dangerous journey.

2. The next person repeats the first sentence, then adds a sentence that follows on from the first to continue the story.

One morning, Joe set out on a dangerous journey. But first he stopped for a bacon sandwich.

TIP: It sometimes helps if you make your story a very weird and random one. Try to picture what's happening at each stage to help you remember, and listen carefully as each player retells it.

(More instructions on the next page)

3. In each player's turn, they must tell the whole story so far from memory, before adding a new sentence at the end.

4. The game ends when someone forgets part of the story, or tells it in the wrong order.

...for a bacon sandwich. The man at the counter was watching T.V.

...was watching T.V. It was the world badminton finals.

...It was the world bowling finals. Oops!

Obstruction

Turn to page 188 for instructions on how to play this game.

Boxes

Turn to page 179 for instructions on how to play this game.

Regions

Turn to page 181 for instructions on how to play this game.

Squiggles

Turn these squiggly shapes into lots of machines that go.

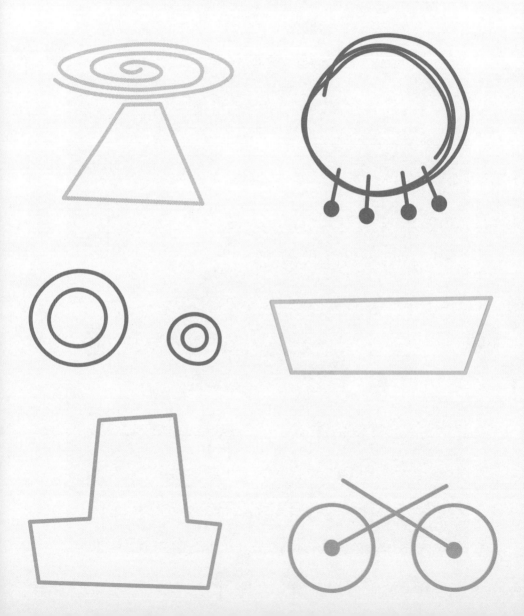

Parking spaces

Drivers often avoid parking their cars too close together. In this game, two players take turns to mark a square for a car. A car cannot be drawn in any of the squares around another car, including diagonals. The first player who can't go loses.

Player 1   Player 2

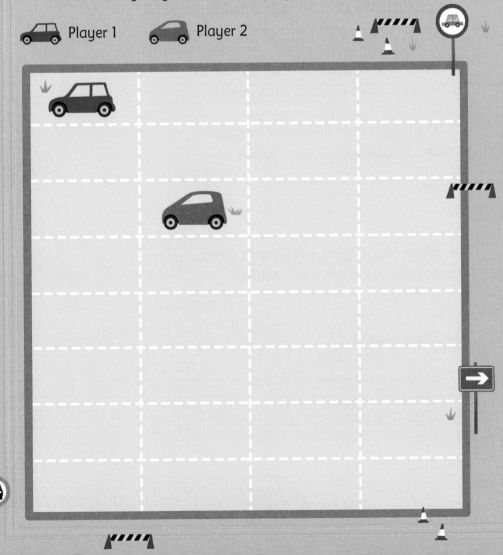

Landmarks quiz

Q1. Which Italian city is famous for its leaning tower?
a) Rome   b) Florence   c) Pisa

**Q2. I turn red at dawn and dusk and weigh 4 million tons.
I am sacred to the local Aboriginal people, who call
me 'Uluru'.** What's my other name?

Q3. What type of building is the Taj Mahal?
a) a temple   b) a fortress   c) a tomb

**Q4. The Empire State Building is the tallest
building in the world.** True or false?

Q5. Who built Stonehenge?
a) Romans   b) Ancient Britons   c) Ancient Greeks

**Q6. Which island, lying in the Pacific Ocean,
is famous for its ancient stone statues?**
a) Easter Island
b) Christmas Island
c) Ascension Island

**Q7. Which country gave the Statue
of Liberty to America as a gift?**
a) France
b) Britain
c) Russia

…grid is made up of six blocks, each containing six squares. Fill in
…x squares so that each block, row and column contains all six le…
…e word ROCKET.

T			R	C	
R			E	T	
	K	O			T
	T	R			E

Woodland road

Find a path through the forest back to your campsite, avoiding the hungry bears and the campfires that block the way.

Start here

Pair them up

Turn to page 184 for instructions on how to play this game.

Stepping stones

Turn to page 178 for instructions on how to play this game.

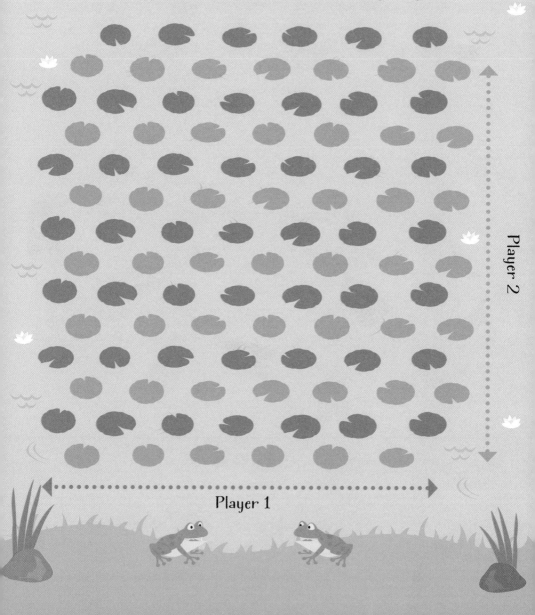

Player 2

Player 1

Vehicle search

Find the names of the vehicles in the grid below.

R	F	R	B	G	A	T	P
E	E	A	W	E	E	R	C
N	R	T	H	B	O	A	T
A	R	R	O	C	N	I	U
L	Y	F	K	O	A	N	G
P	F	E	T	R	C	O	K
L	T	R	R	A	C	S	C
U	E	L	C	Y	C	I	B
C	A	P	L	N	E	F	Z

CAR   BOAT   PLANE   TRAIN   BICYCLE
SCOOTER   CANOE   ROCKET   FERRY

Travel bingo

How quickly can you spot all the things shown below? Cross each one off once you've seen it. To play with a friend, give them the travel bingo from page 90, and race to see who completes their list first.

Black car

Church

Speed limit sign

30

Balloon

Golf course

Train

Horse

School

Cow

Obstruction

Turn to page 188 for instructions on how to play this game.

Treasure hunter

Turn to page 189 for instructions on how to play this game.

Cut or tear along the dotted line.

True or false?

Q1. On a compass, northeast is the opposite direction to southeast.

Q2. One fifth of all the people in the world are Chinese.

Q3. There are planes that can take off on water.

Q4. Rivers flow toward the sea.

Q5. South of the Equator, water spirals down a drain in the opposite direction to north of the Equator.

Q6. More of the Earth is covered by sea than land.

Q7. Passenger jets can fly all the way around the world without stopping.

Q8. Transylvania is a region of Romania.

Q9. Eskimos have over 50 words for snow.

Trains sudoku

This grid is made up of six blocks, each containing six squares. Fill in the blank squares so that each block, row and column contains all six letters of the word TRAINS.

			R	S	
I			R	S	
		T			
	T				n
	R	S			I
n					
			T	A	

Travel bingo

How quickly can you spot all the things shown below? Cross each one off once you've seen it. To play with a friend, give them the travel bingo from page 85, and race to see who completes their list first.

Helicopter

Runner

Wind farm

Fly

Hotel

Ambulance

Street light

Bridge

Flag

Maze master

Turn to page 190 for instructions on how to play this game.

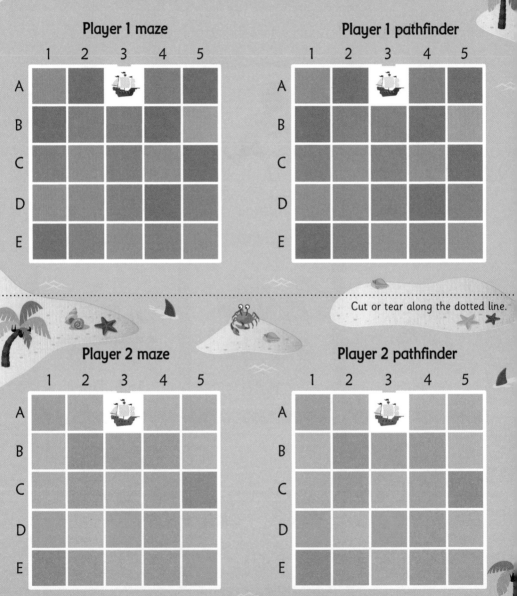

Player 1 maze

Player 1 pathfinder

Cut or tear along the dotted line.

Player 2 maze

Player 2 pathfinder

Boxes

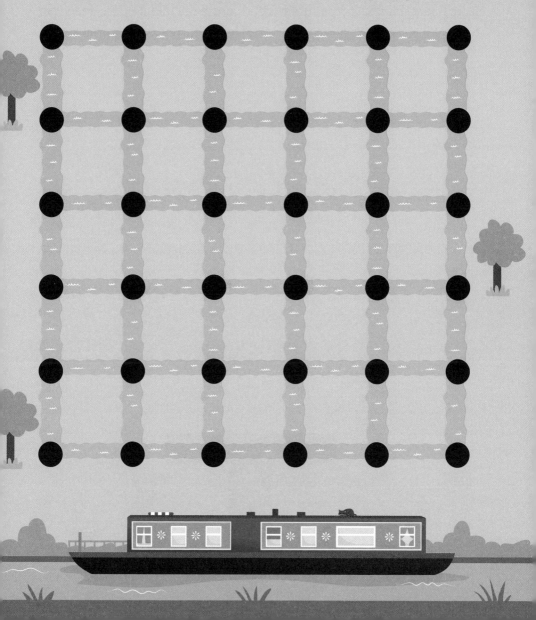

Turn to page 179 for instructions on how to play this game.

Rocket maker

To make a rocket with a friend, tear out this page and fold along the dotted lines. Hiding it from your friend, draw the middle part, then fold it over for them to draw the top part. Unfold to reveal your rocket!

Trip to the farm

This is a game for two or more people.

1. One player begins by saying, "On our trip to the farm, I saw..." followed by the name of an animal. For example, "On our trip to the farm, I saw a horse."

2. The next player must repeat what the first player said, then add another animal, so they might say, "On our trip to the farm, I saw a horse and a hen."

3. Each turn, you must list all of the animals that have already been said, and in the correct order, before saying another, different animal that you saw.

4. The game ends when someone forgets an animal, or says them in the wrong order.

Another idea: You could also say how many of each animal you saw to make the game harder. For example, "On our trip to the farm, I saw eight chicks, six sheep and two pigs."

Word maker

How many new words can you make in two minutes, using the 13 letters of the word below? Once the time is up, add up the total score of all your words – a two letter word scores two points, a three letter word scores three points, and so on.

rollercoaster

Words	Points	Words	Points

Roller COASTER

TOTAL = ...

Memory planes

Look closely at these planes for one minute, then turn to the next page. Can you find them among all the other planes? Turn back to check your answers.

Memory planes

Turn the page over to find out how to play this game.

Target

Turn to page 183 for instructions on how to play this game.

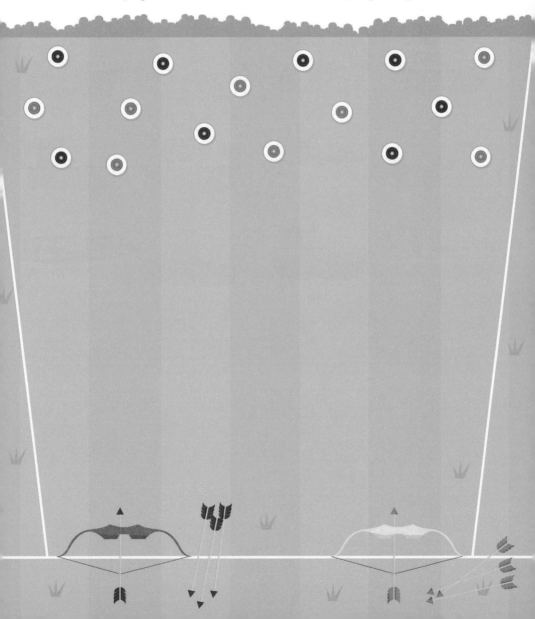

Ship silhouettes

Write each ship's number beneath the silhouette that matches it.

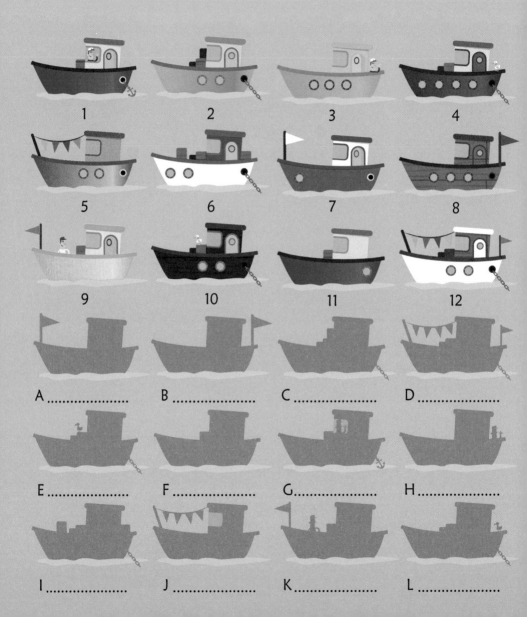

1

2

3

4

5

6

7

8

9

10

11

12

A ....

B ....

C ....

D ....

E ....

F ....

G ....

H ....

I ....

J ....

K ....

L ....

The road

Turn to page 180 for instructions on how to play this game.

Regions

Turn to page 181 for instructions on how to play this game.

Balloon tangle

Which rope should Rachel release to let the balloon take off?

A

B

C

Strike out

Turn to page 182 for instructions on how to play this game.

GAME 1

GAME 2

Circles and squares

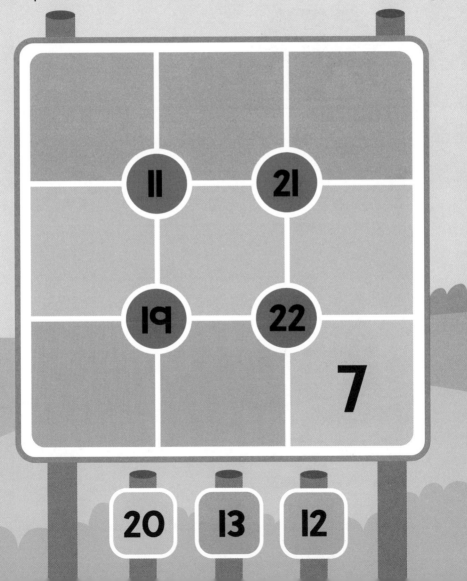

103

Write all the numbers 1 to 9 in the grid, so the four squares around each circle add up to that circle's total, and the orange, blue and purple squares add up to the totals at the bottom. One number has been filled in for you.

11

21

19

22

7

20   13   12

Spot the difference

Can you find and circle **six** differences between these two farmyard scenes?

Travel bingo

How quickly can you spot all the things shown below? Cross each one off once you've seen it. To play with a friend, give them the travel bingo from page 109, and race to see who completes their list first.

Fly	Road repairs	Silver car
Flower	Flag	Bridge
Horse	Clock	Parking area

Explorers timeline

Label these events 1 to 6 to put them into the order they happened, using 1 for the earliest.

Captain James Cook
discovers Australia

Hillary and Tenzing climb
Mount Everest

Roald Amundsen reaches
the South Pole

Yuri Gagarin blasts into space

Neil Armstrong lands
on the Moon

Francis Drake sails
around the world

Try to spot all these things on your journey and mark them off as you go.

- ◯ Bus
- ◯ Church
- ◯ Cow
- ◯ Tent
- ◯ Tree
- ◯ Blue car
- ◯ Duck
- ◯ Ambulance
- ◯ School
- ◯ Plane

- ◯ Stadium
- ◯ Yellow car
- ◯ Lake
- ◯ Store
- ◯ Dog
- ◯ Fire truck
- ◯ Horse
- ◯ Fountain
- ◯ Road repairs
- ◯ Flower

Island regions

Circle the group of
regions that make up
the island on the right.

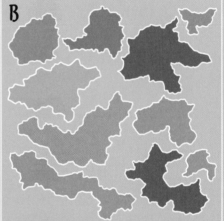

A

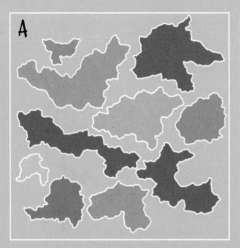

B

C

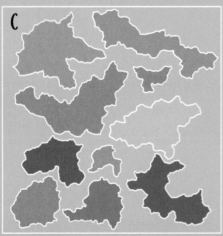

D

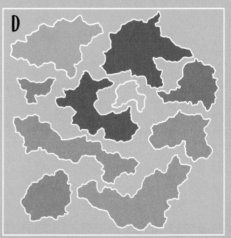

Travel bingo

How quickly can you spot all the things shown below? Cross each one off once you've seen it. To play with a friend, give them the travel bingo from page 105, and race to see who completes their list first.

Traffic cone

Police station

Red car

Plane

Bus stop

Street light

Tractor

Picnic table

River

Maze master

Turn to page 190 for instructions on how to play this game.

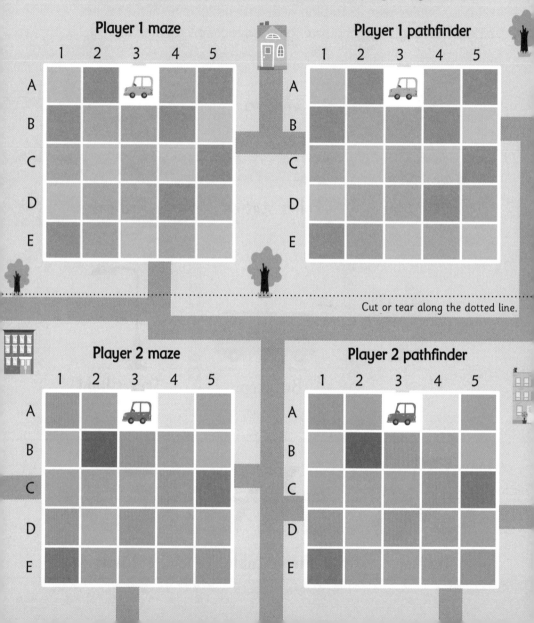

Player 1 maze

Player 1 pathfinder

Cut or tear along the dotted line.

Player 2 maze

Player 2 pathfinder

Fortune teller

Turn to page 191 for instructions on how to fold this page into a fortune teller, then ask it what your destination will be this year.

Cut or tear along the dotted line

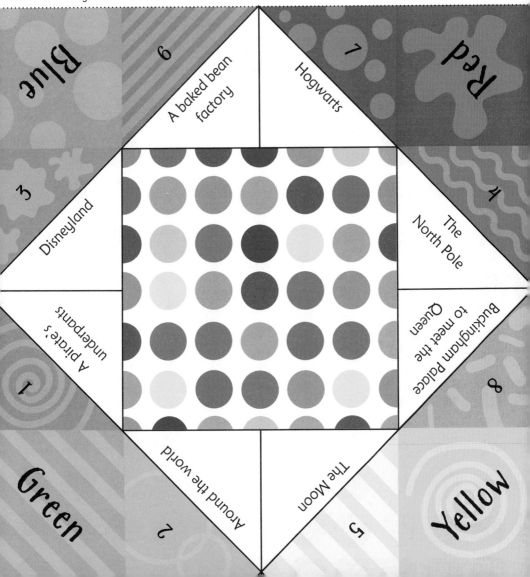

Fortune teller

Scavenger hunt

Try to spot all these things on your journey and mark them off as you go.

◯ Bridge		◯ Silver car	
◯ Skyscraper		◯ Church	
◯ Black car		◯ Balloon	
◯ Road sign		◯ Bicycle	
◯ Bench		◯ Helicopter	
◯ Concrete mixer		◯ Dog	
◯ Boat		◯ Tent	
◯ Barn		◯ House	
◯ Cow		◯ Bird	
◯ Stop sign		◯ Truck	

Hexagon

Turn to page 187 for instructions on how to play this game.

Player 1

Player 2

Player 2

Player 1

Sandcastle switch

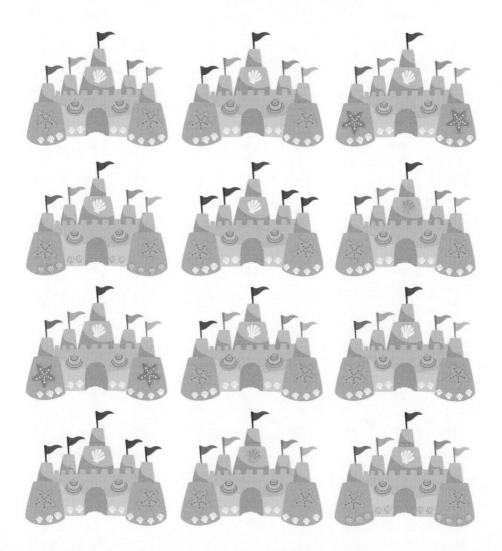

Study these sandcastles carefully for one minute. Now turn to the next page and see if you can circle the two sandcastles that have switched places from memory. Turn back to check your answer.

Sandcastle switch

Turn over the page to find out how to play this game.

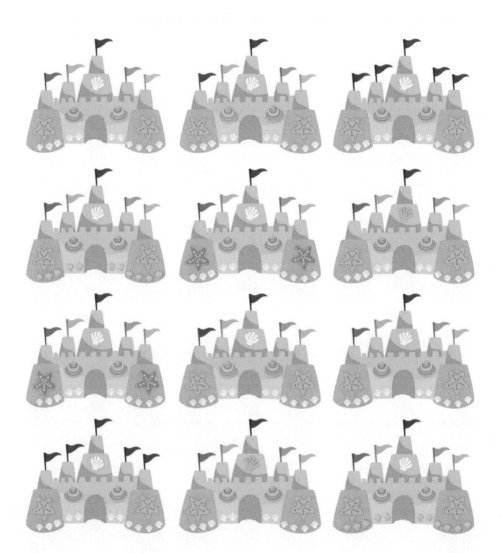

Oh no! But...

This is a game for two or more people.

1. Someone starts the game by saying a sentence that begins "Oh no..." then finishes it by saying something bad. For example, "Oh no, a shark is swimming right at us!"

2. Someone else replies with a sentence that begins "But..." followed by something that stops the situation from being bad. In this example, you could say, "But it's only looking for fish."

3. The game continues with everyone taking turns to add sentences that start with "But..." that take the situation from bad to good and back again. For example, "But I'm eating a tuna sandwich!" "But you can finish it quickly." "But I'll still smell of fish!" And so on.

4. The game ends when someone can't think of anything to add to what the last person has said.

Pair them up

Turn to page 184 for instructions on how to play this game.

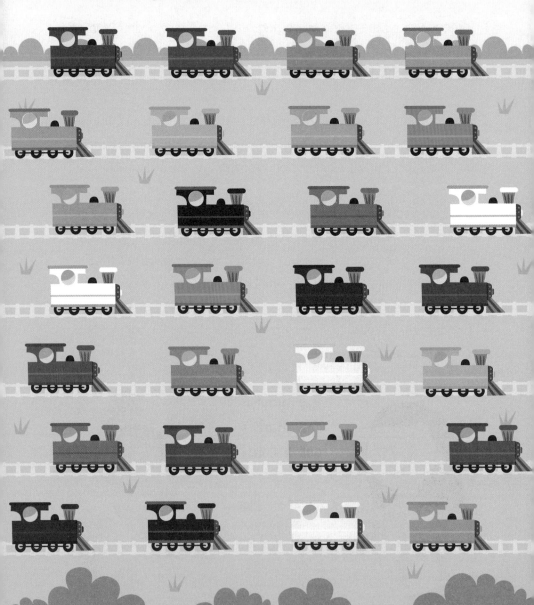

Travel bingo

How quickly can you spot all the things shown below? Cross each one off once you've seen it. To play with a friend, give them the travel bingo from page 134, and race to see who completes their list first.

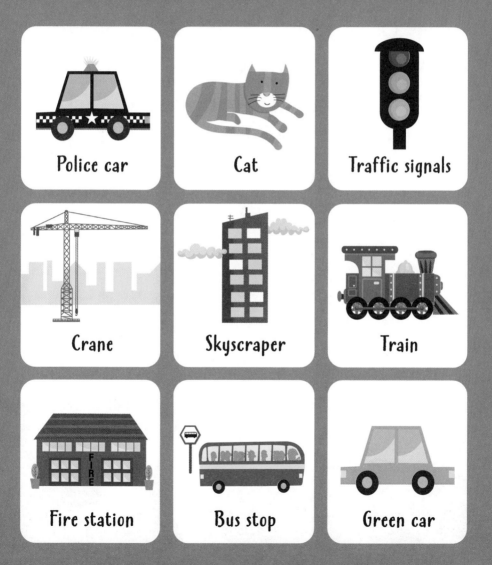

Police car	Cat	Traffic signals
Crane	Skyscraper	Train
Fire station	Bus stop	Green car

City search

Find the names of the famous cities at the bottom in the grid below.

```
S N E H T A R D B O L
H O M P G C E W S U R
J T D I Y N U X P W H
P O R Z V A E L O F D
C Y H E A L Z G U I K
O K R A P B S Q S B W
Y E T M F A U C I O V
N B H O L S R A C R K
I A H G N A H S F I D
B Y U T E C O Z R A L
P A R I S M K E Q N U
```

ATHENS MOSCOW SHANGHAI PERTH NAIROBI PARIS
GLASGOW KYOTO CASABLANCA DENVER

Space crossword

ACROSS

1. planet nearest to the Sun (7)

6. Yuri _____, the first man in space (7)

7. person who goes into space (9)

10. reflective surface (6)

11. our galaxy (5, 3)

DOWN

2. number of planets in the Solar System (5)

3. nickname of NASA's inquisitive Mars rover (9)

4. hurry (3)

5. holes made by meteorites (7)

8. imaginative fiction often set in space (3-2)

9. mixture of gases you breathe on Earth (3)

Paper golf

Turn to page 186 for instructions on how to play this game.

Tee

Travel inventions

Label these inventions 1 to 6 to put them into the order they were first invented, using 1 for the earliest.

Diving suit

Anchor

Radar

Car seat belt

Space suit

Elevator

Regions

Turn to page 181 for instructions on how to play this game.

Boxes

Turn to page 179 for instructions on how to play this game.

Os and Xs

This is a game for two players, played on a 3x3 grid. Player 1 uses Os and Player 2 uses Xs. Take turns drawing your symbol in an empty square. The winner is the player who draws three of their symbols in a straight line. If neither player gets three in a row, the game is a draw.

Scavenger hunt

Try to spot all these things on your journey and mark them off as you go.

○ Train

○ Bush

○ Train station

○ Horse

○ Traffic cone

○ Statue

○ Bus

○ Rainbow

○ Road sign

○ Street light

○ Bridge

○ Balloon

○ Puddle

○ Windmill

○ Red car

○ Tree

○ Bench

○ Green car

○ Crane

○ Fire truck

Strike out

Turn to page 182 for instructions on how to play this game.

GAME 1

GAME 2

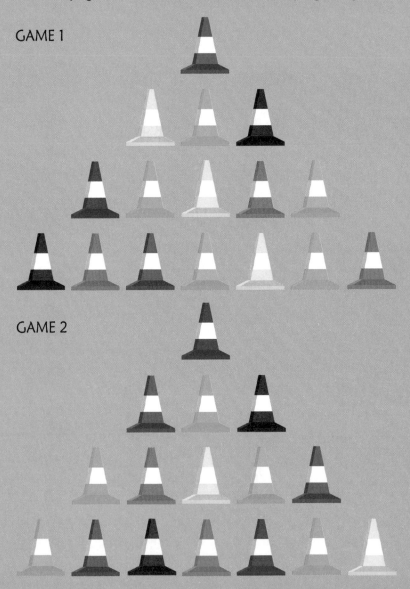

Car shapes

Turn these shapes into cars in a variety of styles and shapes.

Quick draw

Draw a line as quickly as you can so the high-speed train hurtles to the station without leaving the track.

STATION

The road

Turn to page 180 for instructions on how to play this game.

Word maker

How many new words can you make in two minutes, using the ten letters of the word below? Once the time is up, add up the total score of all your words – a two letter word scores two points, a three letter word scores three points, and so on.

lighthouse

Words	Points	Words	Points

TOTAL = ...

Vehicle timeline

Label these vehicles 1 to 9 to put them into the order they were first invented, using 1 for the earliest.

Car

Hovercraft

Submarine

Plane

Space Shuttle

Hot-air balloon

Helicopter

Bicycle

Sailing ship

Hexagon

Turn to page 187 for instructions on how to play this game.

Stepping stones

Turn to page 178 for instructions on how to play this game.

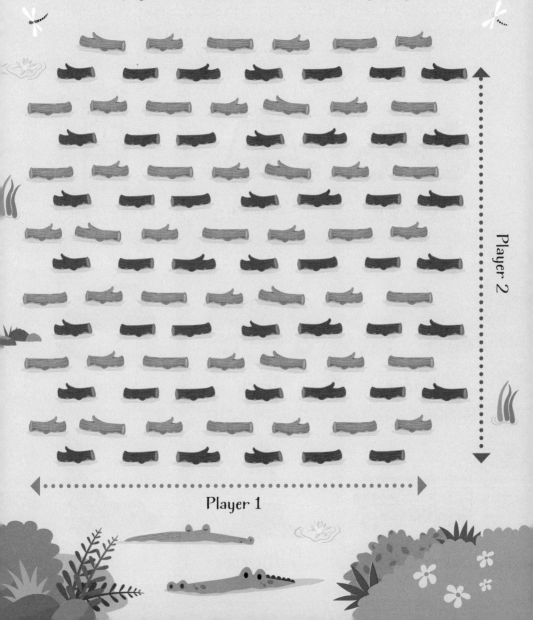

Player 2

Player 1

Travel bingo

How quickly can you spot all the things shown below? Cross each one off once you've seen it. To play with a friend, give them the travel bingo from page 117, and race to see who completes their list first.

Motorcycle

Police car

Skyscraper

Bridge

Truck

Campsite

Fire truck

Traffic cone

Dog

Obstruction

Turn to page 188 for instructions on how to play this game.

Train parts

Circle the group of parts
that make up the train
on the right.

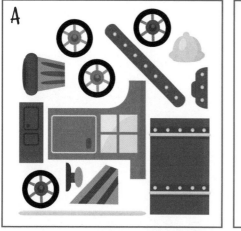

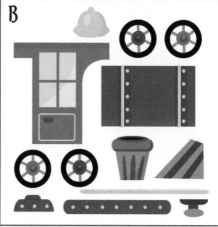

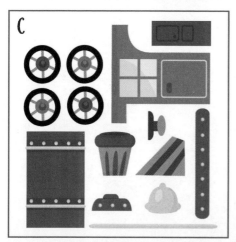

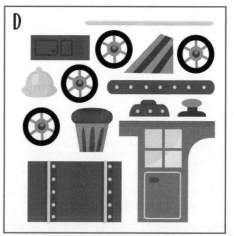

A

B

C

D

Memory vehicles

Look at all the different vehicles below for 30 seconds, then turn the page. How many of them can you write down from memory?

Memory vehicles

Turn over the page to find out how to play this game.

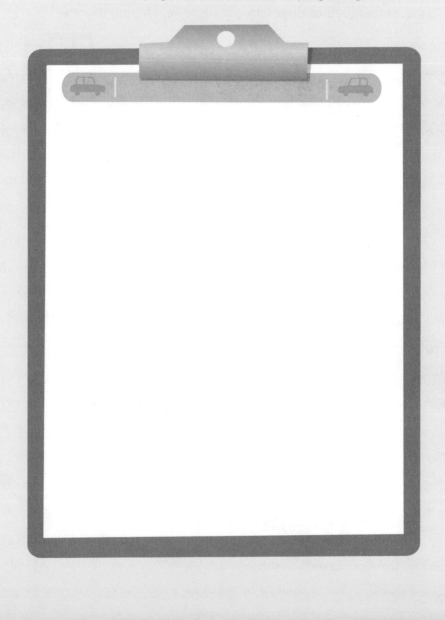

Four in a row

Turn to page 185 for instructions on how to play this game.

The road

Turn to page 180 for instructions on how to play this game.

Pair them up

Turn to page 184 for instructions on how to play this game.

Boxes

Turn to page 179 for instructions on how to play this game.

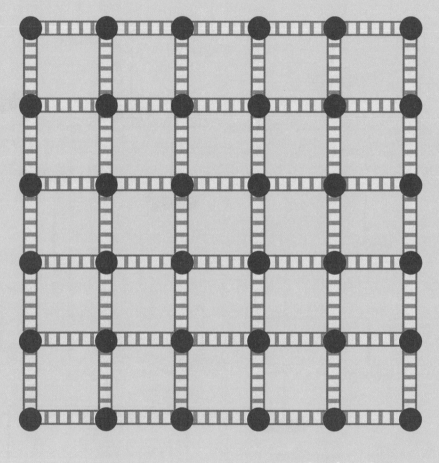

Quick draw

Draw a line as quickly as you can to help the skier race to the bottom of the slope, without leaving the track.

FINISH

Scavenger hunt

Try to spot all these things on your journey and mark them off as you go.

○ Fence

○ Rainbow

○ Fountain

○ Fire truck

○ School

○ Blue car

○ Wind turbine

○ Train station

○ Bridge

○ Phone booth

○ Tunnel

○ Bird

○ Train

○ Balloon

○ Bush

○ Bench

○ Road sign

○ Street light

○ Tent

○ Tree

Paper golf

144

Turn to page 186 for instructions on how to play this game.

Tee

Sailing home

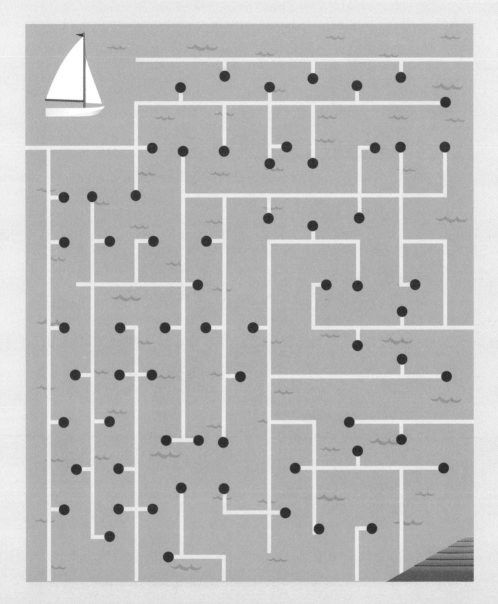

Guide the boat between the lines and buoys to reach the jetty.

Travel bingo

How quickly can you spot all the things shown below? Cross each one off once you've seen it. To play with a friend, give them the travel bingo from page 156, and race to see who completes their list first.

Traffic signals

Crane

Helicopter

Speed limit sign

Roof rack

Statue

Service station

Cow

Forest

Stepping stones

Turn to page 178 for instructions on how to play this game.

Player 2

Player 1

Spot the difference

Can you find and circle **six** differences between the two postcards below?

Hedge maze

Help Carla find her dog, Albert, who's
run off into the middle of this maze.

Hexagon

150

Turn to page 187 for instructions on how to play this game.

Player 1

Player 2

Player 2

Player 1

Circles and squares

Write all the numbers 1 to 9 in the grid, so the four squares around each circle add up to that circle's total, and the purple, yellow and red squares add up to the totals at the bottom. One number has been filled in for you.

Regions

Turn to page 181 for instructions on how to play this game.

Building maker

To make a building with a friend, tear out this page and fold along the dotted lines. Hiding it from your friend, draw the middle part, then fold it over for them to draw the top part. Unfold to reveal your construction!

City shapes

Turn all of these shapes into things you might see in the city.

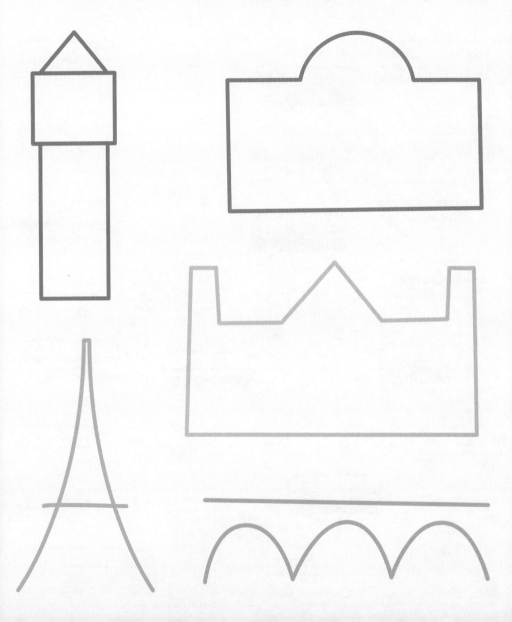

Turn to page 184 for instructions on how to play this game.

Travel bingo

How quickly can you spot all the things shown below? Cross each one off once you've seen it. To play with a friend, give them the travel bingo from page 146, and race to see who completes their list first.

Ambulance

Cat

Farm

Golf course

Black car

Coffee shop

Fire station

Bench

Hills

Strike out

Turn to page 182 for instructions on how to play this game.

GAME 1

GAME 2

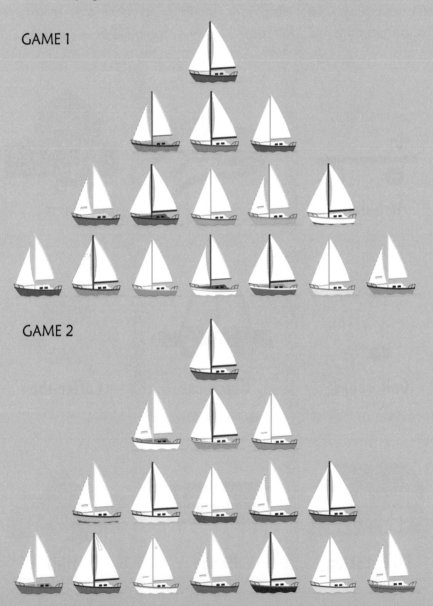

Getting around quiz

Q1. How many wheels does a unicycle have?
a) one   b) two   c) four

Q2. Where was the *Titanic* sailing to when it hit an iceberg and sank?
a) Cape Town   b) New York   c) Liverpool

Q3. Who flew the *Millennium Falcon*?
a) Gandalf   b) Captain America   c) Han Solo

Q4. Which of these is not a famous train?
a) The Flying Scotsman
b) The Orient Express
c) The Spice Trail

Q5. When did the first person land on the Moon?
a) 1929   b) 1969   c) 1999

Q6. Which storybook character flew from England to America in a giant peach carried by seagulls?
a) James   b) Charlie   c) Matilda

Q7. How long does it take to fly non-stop from London to Moscow?
a) two hours   b) four hours   c) eight hours

Scavenger hunt

Try to spot all these things on your journey and mark them off as you go.

○ Tractor

○ Tree

○ Ambulance

○ Dog

○ Wind turbine

○ Helicopter

○ Bush

○ Stadium

○ Road repairs

○ Black car

○ Horse

○ Skyscraper

○ Duck

○ Church

○ Concrete mixer

○ Road sign

○ Tent

○ Lake

○ Bus

○ Silver car

Memory vehicles

Look at all the vehicles in this picture for 30 seconds, then turn the page.
How many of them can you write down from memory?

Memory vehicles

Turn over the page to find out how to play this game.

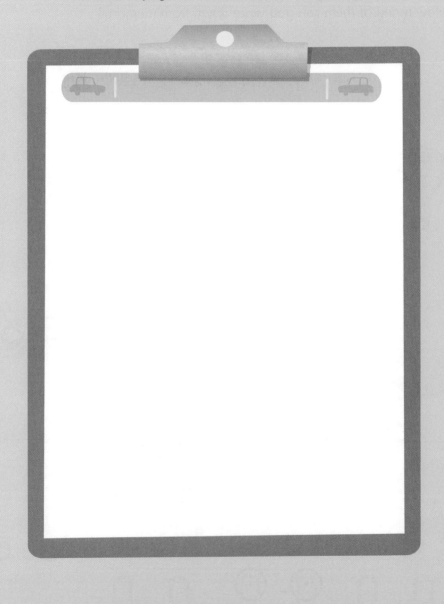

The road

Turn to page 180 for instructions on how to play this game.

Maize maze

Guide the farmer's tractor back between the high walls of corn to the barn in the middle of the field.

Travel bingo

How quickly can you spot all the things shown below? Cross each one off once you've seen it. To play with a friend, give them the travel bingo from page 171, and race to see who completes their list first.

Satellite dish

Church

Cow

School

Tractor

Wind farm

Green car

Balloon

Train crossing

CROSSING

Pair them up

Turn to page 184 for instructions on how to play this game.

Scavenger hunt

Try to spot all these things on your journey and mark them off as you go.

◯ Gate	◯ Stop sign
◯ Red car	◯ Service station
◯ Plane	◯ Tent
◯ Traffic signals	◯ Cow
◯ Yellow car	◯ Bird
◯ Bridge	◯ Police car
◯ Truck	◯ Boat
◯ Barn	◯ Bicycle
◯ House	◯ Store
◯ Motorcycle	◯ Flower

Treasure hunter

Turn to page 189 for instructions on how to play this game.

Cut or tear along the dotted line.

Hexagon

Turn to page 187 for instructions on how to play this game.

Player 1

Player 2

Player 2

Player 1

Suitcase squiggles

Turn the squiggles below into things you might pack in your travel bag.

Regions

Turn to page 181 for instructions on how to play this game.

Treasure hunter

Turn to page 189 for instructions on how to play this game.

Cut or tear along the dotted line.

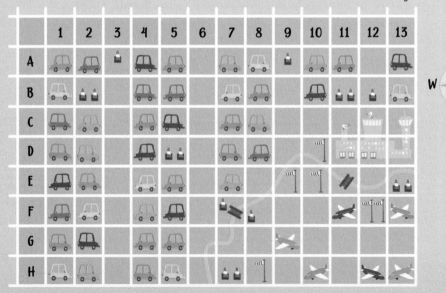

Travel bingo

How quickly can you spot all the things shown below? Cross each one off once you've seen it. To play with a friend, give them the travel bingo from page 163, and race to see who completes their list first.

Wind farm

Bird

Runner

River

Supermarket

Tow truck

Hotel

Stop sign

Blue car

Obstruction

Turn to page 188 for instructions on how to play this game.

Quick draw

Draw a line as quickly as you can to speed to the lake without crashing the kayak into the rocks or the riverbank.

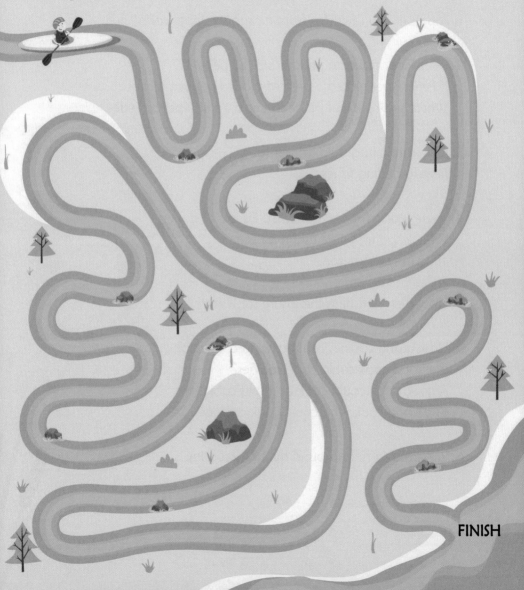

FINISH

Tongue twisters

Try to say each of these tongue twisters as fast as you can.

1. A proper cup of coffee from a proper copper coffee pot.

2. Peter Piper picked a peck of pickled pepper.
   If Peter Piper picked a peck of pickled pepper,
   Where's the peck of pickled pepper Peter Piper picked?

3. Five frantic frogs fled from fifty
   fiercely flailing fishes.

4. There was a fisherman named Fisher,
   Who fished for some fish in a fissure,
   Till a fish with a grin,
   Pulled the fisherman in.
   Now they're fishing the fissure for Fisher.

5. How many cookies could a good cook cook
   if a good cook could cook cookies?
   A good cook could cook as many cookies
   as a good cook who could cook cookies.

6. Roberta ran rings around the Roman ruins.

Turn to page 186 for instructions on how to play this game.

Tee

The road

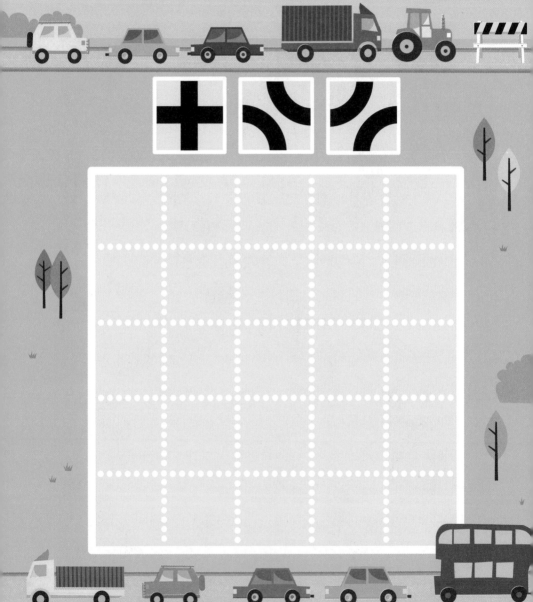

Turn to page 180 for instructions on how to play this game.

Boat, sea, fish

This is a game for two or more people.

1. To start, someone chooses a word, then says it out loud. For example, you could say "boat" as the first word.

2. Someone else then says a word they associate with the first word. For instance, the word "boat" might make them think of the word "sea" in this example.

3. The next person says a word that they associate with the word that has just been said. After "sea" the next person might say "fish" or "seaweed" or something else that lives in the sea. That might lead on to "scales" or "slimy" or "green" and so on.

4. The game continues with everyone taking turns to say a word. If anyone pauses, or repeats a word that's already been said, they lose, and the game starts again with a new word.

Stepping stones instructions 178

For pages 17, 46, 83, 133, 147

1 Player 1 starts by connecting two of the blue stones together using a horizontal or vertical straight line.

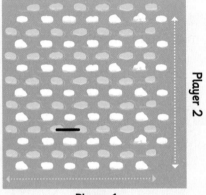

Player 2

Player 1

2 Player 2 then connects two of the white stones together using a horizontal or vertical straight line.

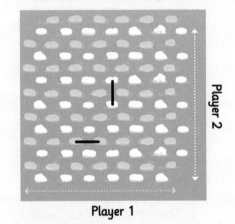

Player 2

Player 1

3 Taking turns, connect two of your stones anywhere on the grid. But you can't cross a line that's already been made.

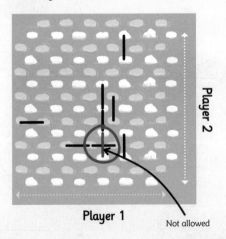

Player 2

Player 1   Not allowed

4 The first player to cross the grid is the winner. Player 1's chain must cross from side to side, and Player 2's from top to bottom.

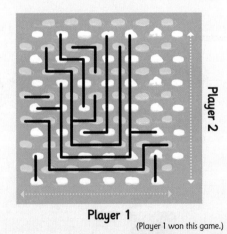

Player 2

Player 1

(Player 1 won this game.)

Boxes instructions

For pages 7, 75, 92, 123, 141

1 Player 1 (red) joins any two dots with a horizontal or vertical straight line.

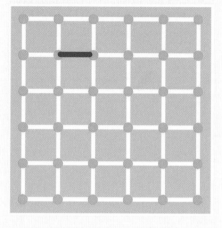

2 Player 2 (blue) then makes another horizontal or vertical straight line.

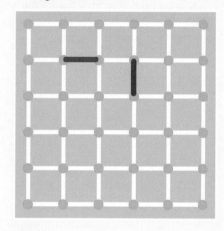

3 Each turn you try to complete as many boxes as you can. When you complete a box, write your initial inside and take an extra turn.

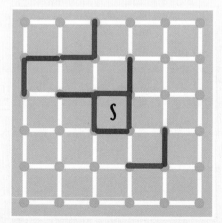

4 When no more lines can be added, the winner is the player who's made the most boxes. Player 1 won this game.

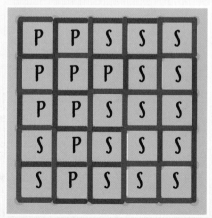

The road instructions

For pages 15, 30, 99, 129, 139, 161, 176

1 Player 1 (blue) chooses one of the three tiles above and draws it in the top left square of the grid.

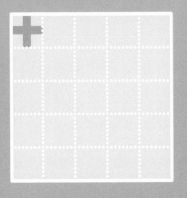

2 Player 2 (red) then selects one of the tiles and draws it in a joining square to continue the road.

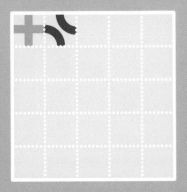

3 Take turns choosing tiles that extend the road without forcing it off the grid.

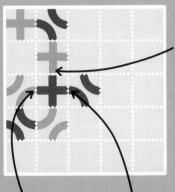

At junctions, the road must exit on the opposite side to the one it entered on.

If a tile links the road to an existing section...

...the next move continues from the end of that section.

4 If you play a tile that links the road to the edge of the grid, you lose the game. Player 1 won this game.

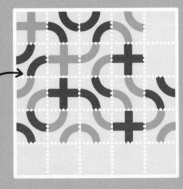

Player 2 lost because this tile joins the road to a section that touches the grid's edge.

Regions instructions

For pages 9, 59, 76, 100, 122, 152, 169

1 Player 1 shades any region of the map with horizontal stripes.

2 Player 2 then shades any other region with vertical stripes.

3 Take turns shading regions with your stripes. You can't shade any region that borders one that you've already shaded.

4 The first player who can't shade a new region loses the game. Red won this game, as blue has nowhere to go.

Strike out instructions

For pages 11, 102, 126, 157

1 Player 1 (red) chooses a row, and crosses out some of its cones. You can cross out as many cones as you want, but only from that row.

2 Player 2 (blue) then chooses a row and crosses out some of its cones. You can choose the same row as Player 1, or a different row.

3 The winner is the player who crosses out the last cone.

4 Player 2 won this game.

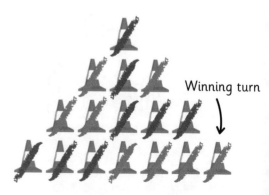

Winning turn

Target instructions

For pages 36, 97

1 Before the game begins, each player chooses a rocket. This is your starting position for the rest of the game.

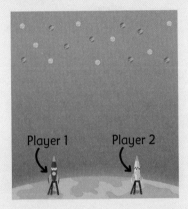

2 The goal is to reach a planet by drawing a straight line in one quick swipe. Here, Player 1 aims at the red planets, Player 2 at the yellow.

3 Score a point for each planet you hit. But if you also hit your opponent's planet with the same line, score zero points. If you hit two of your own planets, score two points.

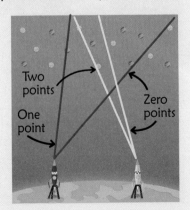

4 The first player to score three points is the winner. If both players reach three points in the same number of turns, the game is a tie. Player 2 won this game.

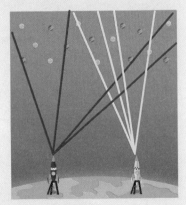

Pair them up instructions

For pages 3, 67, 82, 116, 140, 155, 164

1 Player 1 (blue) draws a line between any matching pair.

2 Player 2 (green) then draws a line between any other matching pair.

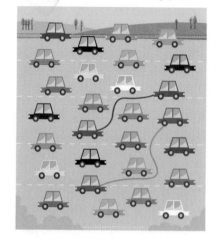

3 You must draw your line without taking your pen off the page. If it touches a car from a different pair, or another line, you lose the game.

4 Player 2 won this game, because Player 1 touched another line while trying to join the two orange cars.

touching lines

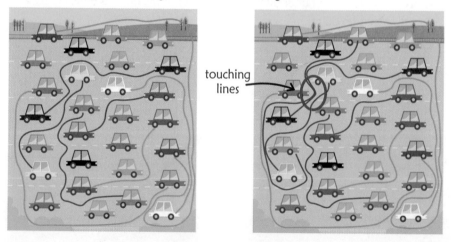

Four in a row instructions 185

For pages 41, 61, 66, 138

1 Player 1 starts by drawing an X in any circle on the bottom row.

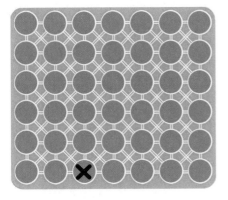

2 Player 2 then draws an O in any of the other circles on the bottom row, or in the circle above the X.

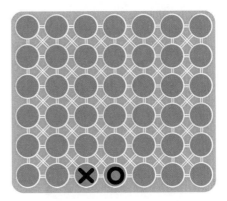

3 You can draw your symbol in any column you like, but you must always draw it in the column's lowest empty circle.

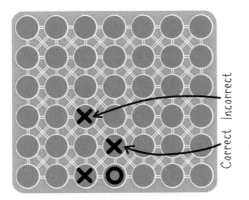

Correct Incorrect

4 The first player to make a straight line of four is the winner. The line can be horizontal, vertical or diagonal. Player 1 won this game.

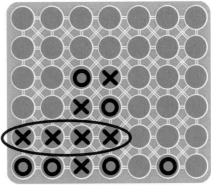

Paper golf instructions

For pages 33, 120, 144, 175

1 This is a game for 1–4 players. First, plan your route from the tee to the pin, then Player 1 puts their pen on the tee and closes their eyes.

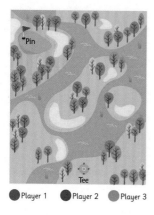

Player 1   Player 2   Player 3

2 Player 1 draws a straight line along their planned route, keeping their eyes closed until they take their pen off the page.

3 If your line hits a tree, take your next shot from where you hit the tree. If you land in sand take your next shot as normal, but if you land in water, take your next shot from your last position.

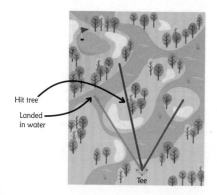

Hit tree
Landed in water

4 The winner is the player who gets their ball in the hole in the fewest turns. If two or more players take the same number of turns, the game is drawn. Player 1 won this game.

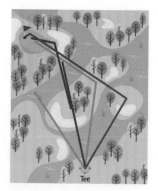

Hexagon instructions

For pages 24, 65, 113, 132, 150, 167

1 Player 1 (blue) fills in one of the hexagons on the grid.

2 Player 2 (red) then fills in any of the other hexagons on the grid.

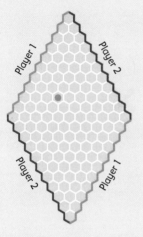

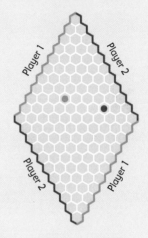

3 Taking turns, fill in hexagons anywhere on the grid. The goal is to make a chain that connects your two sides of the grid.

4 The winner is the first player to make a complete chain. Player 1 won this game.

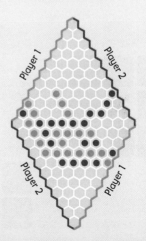

Obstruction instructions

For pages 53, 74, 86, 135, 172

1 Player 1 marks their symbol in any of the squares in the grid.

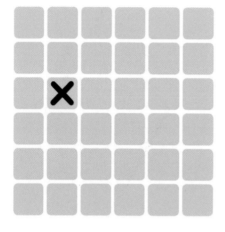

2 Player 2 then marks their symbol in another square in the grid.

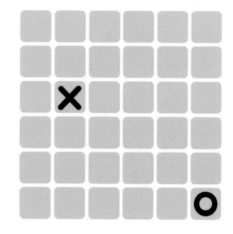

3 You can't place your mark in a square that touches another marked square. So, all of the squares shaded red are off limits.

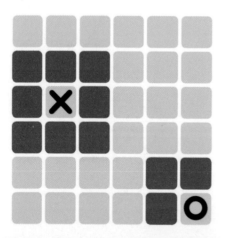

4 Take it in turns until there are no free squares left. The player who makes the last mark is the winner. Player 1 won this game.

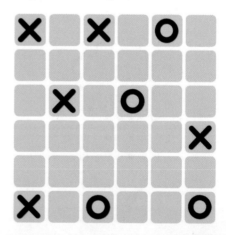

Treasure hunter instructions

For pages 27, 49, 72, 87, 166, 170

Before you start, cut or tear along the dotted line so you both have a
map. Then secretly mark your treasure in one of the squares with an X.

1 Now take turns searching for your opponent's treasure. You can either
guess the square it's on…

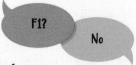

Player 1 map

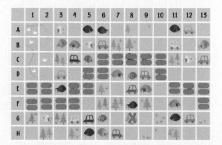

Player 2 map

2 …or ask a yes/no question to narrow the search.

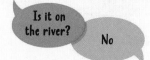

Player 1 map

Player 2 map

3 You can also use features on the map to help you in your search.

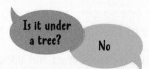

Player 1 map

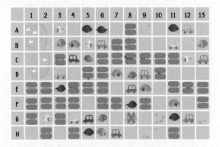

Player 2 map

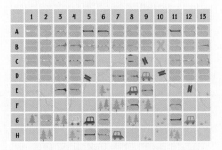

4 The first player to find their opponent's treasure is the winner.

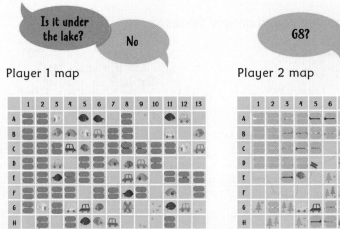

Maze master instructions

190

For pages 35, 71, 91, 110

1 Each player writes an X in any empty square on their maze grid. This marks the spot where their treasure is hidden. Make sure the other player never sees this grid.

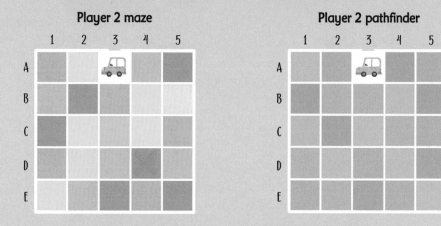

2 Now each player creates a maze by drawing fifteen walls on their maze grid. You can only join three walls in a straight line, and none of the squares on your grid can be completely blocked off.

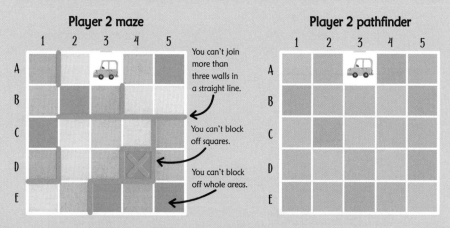

You can't join more than three walls in a straight line.

You can't block off squares.

You can't block off whole areas.

3 You start the game on square A3. Each turn, you can move one, two or three squares in a straight line, either vertically or horizontally. If your move is blocked by a wall, your opponent tells you to stop at the wall. Draw both your move and the wall on your pathfinder grid. Draw your opponent's moves on your maze grid.

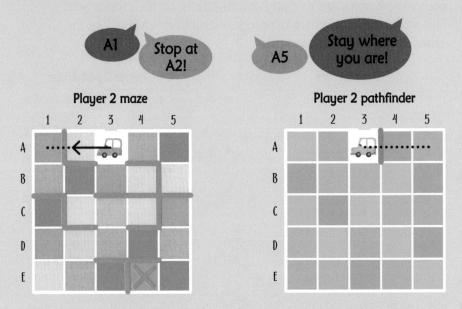

4 Take turns calling out your moves. The winner is the first player to land on (or pass through) their opponent's treasure. Player 1 won this game.

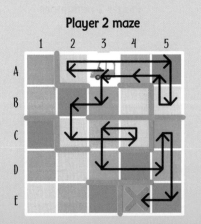

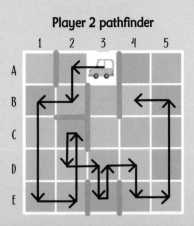

Maze master instructions

For pages 35, 71, 91, 110

1 Each player writes an X in any empty square on their maze grid.
   This marks the spot where their treasure is hidden. Make sure the
   other player never sees this grid.

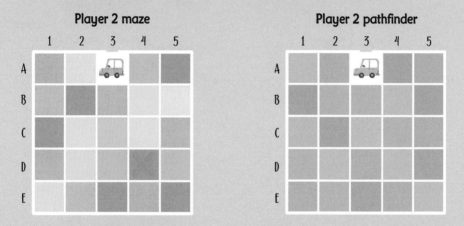

Player 2 maze

Player 2 pathfinder

2 Now each player creates a maze by drawing fifteen walls on their maze
   grid. You can only join three walls in a straight line, and none of the
   squares on your grid can be completely blocked off.

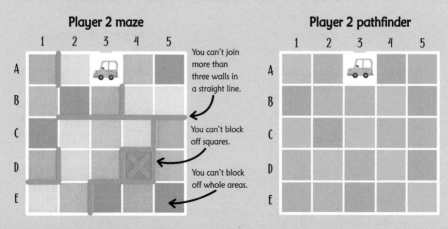

Player 2 maze

Player 2 pathfinder

You can't join
more than
three walls in
a straight line.

You can't block
off squares.

You can't block
off whole areas.

3 You start the game on square A3. Each turn, you can move one, two or three squares in a straight line, either vertically or horizontally. If your move is blocked by a wall, your opponent tells you to stop at the wall. Draw both your move and the wall on your pathfinder grid. Draw your opponent's moves on your maze grid.

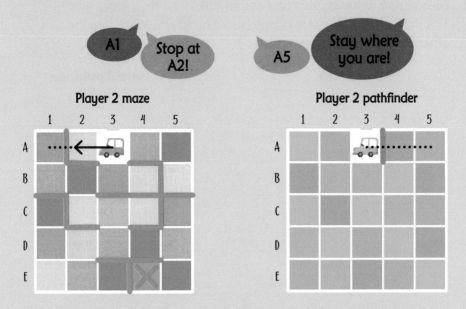

4 Take turns calling out your moves. The winner is the first player to land on (or pass through) their opponent's treasure. Player 1 won this game.

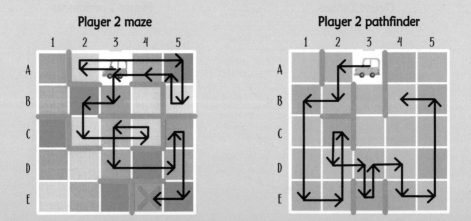

Answers

42 Geography quiz

1. b; 2. b; 3. b, c, a; 4. c; 5. back; 6. a; 7. a

43 Circles and squares

45 Shoreline challenge

47 Spot the difference

50 Vehicle sudoku

57 Sand search

58 Car silhouettes

A8; B4; C10; D5; E11; F12;
G3; H9; I1; J6; K7; L2

62 Skiing crossword

64 Across the ice

68 Spot the difference

Answers

69 Train track

79 Landmarks quiz

1. c; 2. Ayers Rock; 3. c;
4. False; 5. b; 6. a; 7. a

80 Rocket sudoku

T	E	K	R	C	O
K	C	T	O	E	R
R	O	C	E	T	K
E	K	O	C	R	T
O	R	E	T	K	C
C	T	R	K	O	E

81 Woodland road

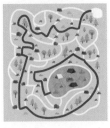

84 Vehicle search

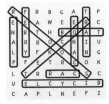

88 True or false?

1. false (it's southwest); 2. true; 3. true; 4. true;
5. false; 6. true; 7. false; 8. true; 9. false

89 Trains sudoku

I	n	A	R	S	T
R	S	T	n	I	A
A	T	I	S	R	n
T	R	S	A	n	I
n	A	R	I	T	S
S	I	n	T	A	R

98 Ship silhouettes

A7, B8, C2, D12, E10, F11,
G1, H3, I6, J5, K9, L4

101 Balloon tangle: C

103 Circles and squares

104 Spot the difference

106 Explorers timeline

1. Drake 1577–1580; 2. Cook 1770;
3. South Pole 1911; 4. Everest 1953;
5. Gagarin 1961; 6. Moon 1969

108 Island regions: D